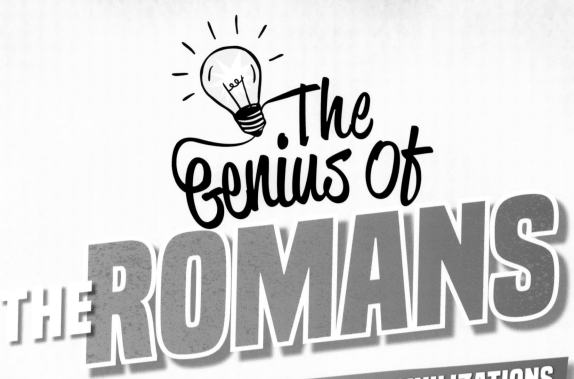

The Genius Of THE ROMANS

INNOVATIONS FROM PAST CIVILIZATIONS

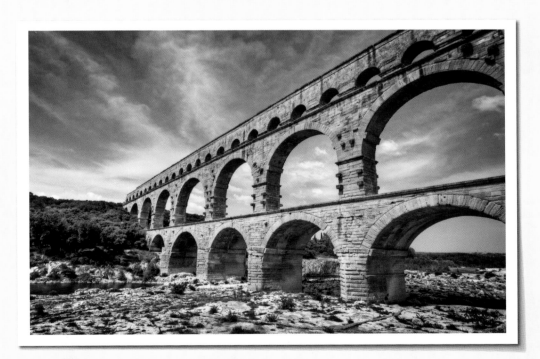

IZZI HOWELL

CRABTREE
PUBLISHING COMPANY
WWW.CRABTREEBOOKS.COM

CRABTREE
PUBLISHING COMPANY
WWW.CRABTREEBOOKS.COM

Published in Canada
Crabtree Publishing
616 Welland Avenue
St. Catharines, ON
L2M 5V6

Published in the United States
Crabtree Publishing
PMB 59051
350 Fifth Ave, 59th Floor
New York, NY 10118

Published in 2020 by Crabtree Publishing Company

Author: Izzi Howell

Editorial director: Kathy Middleton

Editors: Izzi Howell, Petrice Custance

Proofreader: Melissa Boyce

Series Designer: Rocket Design (East Anglia) Ltd

Prepress technician: Tammy McGarr

Print coordinator: Katherine Berti

Consultant: Philip Parker

Photo credits:
Alamy: Chronicle 15b, North Wind Picture Archives 17, Atlaspix 22, nicoolay 27, The Print Collector 29; Getty: 1001nights cover, Neil Holmes 6, DEA / G. DAGLI ORTI/De Agostini 9t, mmac72 10, georgeclerk 11, ANDREAS SOLARO/AFP 14, Aksenovko 15t, AndreaAstes 16, DEA / L. PEDICINI 19b, Stefano Bianchetti/Corbis 25; Shutterstock: Lagui 3, McCarthy's PhotoWorks 4l, rusty426 4r, Sopotnicki 5b, Marco Ossino 9b, Brian Maudsley 12, bigacis 18t, MIGUEL GARCIA SAAVEDRA 18c, Volosina 18bl, baibaz 18br, eFesenko 19t, Mirec 20, Giakita 21, Kamira 23, S.Borisov 24, Algol 26t, J. Lekavicius 26b, meunierd 28, Marco Rubino 30.

All design elements from Shutterstock.

Every attempt has been made to clear copyright. Should there be any inadvertent omission please apply to the publisher for rectification.

Printed in the U.S.A./072019/CG20190501

Library and Archives Canada Cataloguing in Publication

Title: The genius of the Romans / Izzi Howell.
Names: Howell, Izzi, author.
Series: Genius of the ancients.
Description: Series statement: The genius of the ancients | Includes index.
Identifiers: Canadiana (print) 20190108487 | Canadiana (ebook) 20190108517 | ISBN 9780778765769 (hardcover) | ISBN 9780778765967 (softcover) | ISBN 9781427123930 (HTML)
Subjects: LCSH: Rome—Civilization—Juvenile literature. | LCSH: Technological innovations—Rome— Juvenile literature.
Classification: LCC DG77 .H69 2019 | DDC j937—dc23

Library of Congress Cataloging-in-Publication Data

Names: Howell, Izzi, author.
Title: The genius of the Romans / Izzi Howell.
Description: New York, New York : Crabtree Publishing Company, 2020. Series: The genius of the ancients | Audience: Ages: 9-12. | Audience: Grades: 4-6. | Includes index. |
Identifiers: LCCN 2019014240 (print) | LCCN 2019018664 (ebook) | ISBN 9781427123930 (Electronic) | ISBN 9780778765769 (hardcover) | ISBN 9780778765967 (pbk.)
Subjects: LCSH: Rome--Civilization--Juvenile literature. | Technological innovations--Rome--Juvenile literature.
Classification: LCC DG77 (ebook) | LCC DG77 .H69 2020 (print) | DDC 937--dc23
LC record available at https://lccn.loc.gov/2019014240

CONTENTS

THE ROMANS

Who?

The Romans were one of the greatest **civilizations** of all time. It began around 1000 B.C.E. with a group of Latin-speaking people who lived on the banks of the Tiber River, which flows through the city of Rome in Italy. By 600 B.C.E., Rome was an important **city-state** ruled by kings. The Romans then went through different stages of rule. First, there was the Roman **Republic**, followed by the Roman **Empire** and the rule of emperors. The Romans conquered land across Europe, the Middle East, and North Africa, spreading their **culture** and leaving a **legacy** that lives on today.

Romans carried banners such as this one into battle. "SPQR" stands for "the Roman Senate and people" in Latin.

According to **myths**, the twins Romulus and Remus were the founders of the city of Rome. In the story, the twins were raised by a wolf after their parents abandoned them.

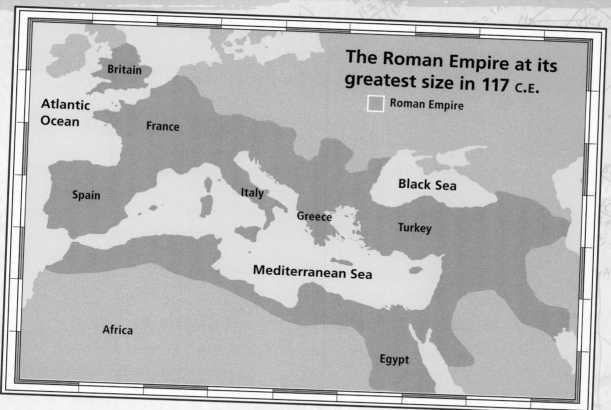

The Roman Empire at its greatest size in 117 C.E.

☐ Roman Empire

Britain

Atlantic Ocean

France

Spain

Italy

Greece

Black Sea

Turkey

Mediterranean Sea

Africa

Egypt

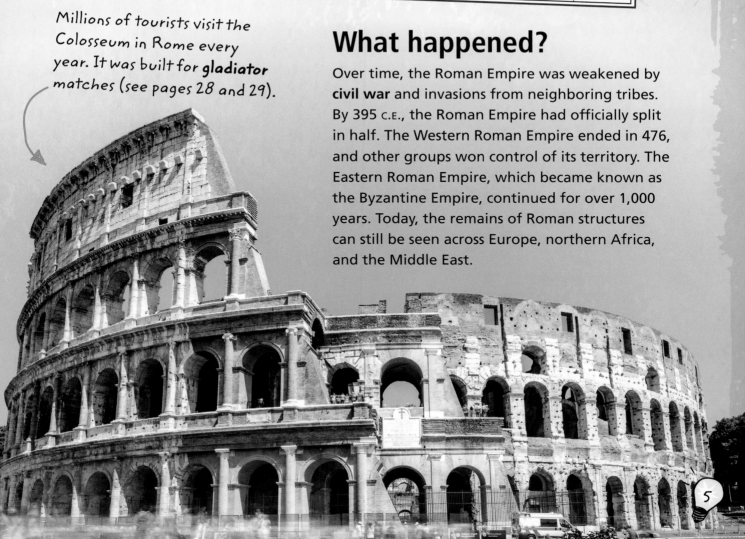

Millions of tourists visit the Colosseum in Rome every year. It was built for **gladiator** matches (see pages 28 and 29).

What happened?

Over time, the Roman Empire was weakened by **civil war** and invasions from neighboring tribes. By 395 C.E., the Roman Empire had officially split in half. The Western Roman Empire ended in 476, and other groups won control of its territory. The Eastern Roman Empire, which became known as the Byzantine Empire, continued for over 1,000 years. Today, the remains of Roman structures can still be seen across Europe, northern Africa, and the Middle East.

THE ARMY

GENIUS ★ PROFESSIONAL SOLDIERS

The large and organized Roman army was key to the expansion of its empire. Around 30 B.C.E., the Roman army went from being strong to being unbeatable. This was due to one major change—being a soldier became a full-time job.

Volunteer to professional

Ancient armies were made up of volunteer soldiers, who only fought when needed. They provided their own weapons and uniform. However, professional soldiers in the Roman army were committed to military life. They signed up for around 20 years of service and received a salary. The army provided their armor and weapons so that everyone was equally prepared for battle.

These actors show how Roman soldiers held their shields to protect themselves from enemy spears and arrows.

Training

Having a professional army constantly ready for battle made it worthwhile for the Romans to spend money on training their soldiers. New army members had to train hard, learn to follow commands, work as a team, and practice fighting with swords and **javelins**. A Roman soldier was expected to walk 19 miles (30 km) a day in full armor and build a new camp every evening.

Into battle

The soldiers' training and preparation paid off on the battlefield. Rather than running straight into battle, soldiers, **archers**, and **cavalry** moved **tactically**, working together to take down the enemy. Thanks to their hours of practice, they knew how to quickly get into different military **formations** on the command of their leaders.

BATTLE PLANS

The army's tactics depended on the size and strength of the enemy and the land of the battlefield.

enemy troops

Roman soldiers

enemy troops

Roman soldiers

enemy troops

Roman soldiers

① **Wedge formation**
The soldiers are concentrated in the center to break through enemy lines.

② **Single-line defense**
The soldiers are arranged in a single line that wraps around enemy troops.

③ **Weak center**
Only a few soldiers are placed in the center to tempt the enemy to attack there. Then the other soldiers move in on either side.

(((BRAIN WAVE)))

In the tortoise formation, soldiers packed together tightly to form a square, using their shields like a tortoiseshell to protect their sides and heads. The result was an **impenetrable** block of soldiers moving together without getting hurt by the enemy.

TRADE

The Romans controlled many different areas. They conquered these lands to expand their empire and power. Their huge gains in territory came with the added bonus of access to **natural resources**.

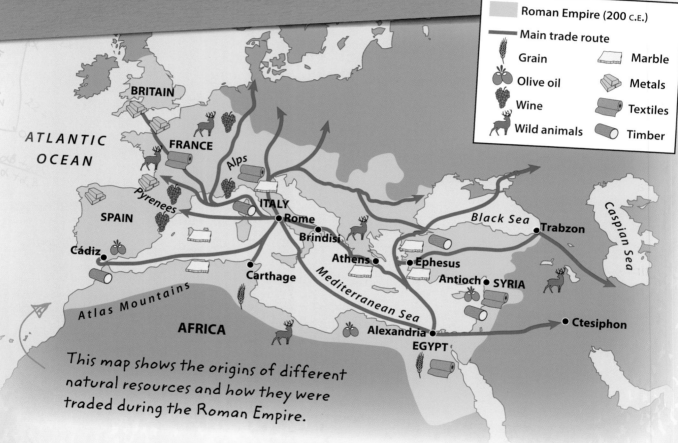

Roman Empire (200 C.E.)	
Main trade route	
Grain	Marble
Olive oil	Metals
Wine	Textiles
Wild animals	Timber

This map shows the origins of different natural resources and how they were traded during the Roman Empire.

Across the empire

Roman territory included areas with different **climates** and types of land. Some natural resources, such as lead, could only be found in certain areas, such as Britain and Spain. The Romans transported this lead to Italy, where it was used to construct water pipes in Rome. Other regions had climates that were well suited to growing certain crops. Farmers in North Africa grew wheat that was taken across the empire and used to make bread.

Road or sea

The wide-reaching Roman road network (see pages 12 to 13) made it easier for traders to move items around the empire. However, the Romans learned it could sometimes be cheaper and quicker to send products across the Mediterranean Sea. They built large ports where products could be received and sent inland. The port of Ostia was built on the coast near Rome to supply the city with trade goods.

Luxury goods

Roman traders established trade connections beyond their empire, giving them access to an even wider range of products. Traders sailed across the Indian Ocean to India, bringing back luxury items such as silk, perfume, pepper, and cinnamon. The time and effort required to collect these items would have made them extremely expensive.

(((BRAIN WAVE)))

Pirates often disrupted trade in the Mediterranean Sea. This could affect food supply across the empire. In 67 B.C.E., the politician Pompey was given control over the Mediterranean Sea and coastline, and a large fleet of ships to fight the pirates. He defeated them in just a few months.

This picture shows the Roman god Dionysus fighting off pirates.

The Romans also traded wild animals with India. This Roman artwork shows tigers, which can only be found in Asia. Tigers were brought to Italy for gladiator shows.

CONCRETE

The Romans developed a new recipe for concrete which was strong and **versatile**. They used this concrete to construct arched **aqueducts** and bridges, as well as massive domed roofs.

A Roman recipe

Roman concrete was made from small chunks of rock held together by **mortar** made with volcanic ash and seawater. This mixture set into a hard block that wasn't just resistant to damage, but actually got stronger over time when placed in the sea. Modern scientists have discovered that mixing volcanic ash with seawater will create new **minerals** that fill in any cracks in the concrete. Some types of Roman concrete could even set underwater, making it an ideal material for harbors, bridges, and sewers.

The Romans used volcanic ash mortar to bind together the top blocks of the Pont du Gard aqueduct in the south of France. The rest of the blocks were cut so accurately that they didn't need mortar to stay in place.

New shapes

Roman concrete could be poured into **molds** to create building blocks in any shape. Previously, builders had to chisel pieces of stone down to size, which was time-consuming and required high levels of skill. The Romans didn't like the appearance of concrete, so they covered concrete blocks in bricks or stone.

Daring domes

The greatest Roman concrete dome is located in the Pantheon temple in Rome. Built between 118 and 125 C.E., the dome is 141 feet (43 m) in diameter and 72 feet (22 m) tall. It is supported only by the wall beneath it. Previously, domes were supported by pillars, taking up a lot of space inside the building. The inside of the Pantheon is a huge, open space, with the domed roof rising unsupported above.

This oculus, or hole, in the ceiling of the Pantheon lets natural light stream into the building.

TEST OF TIME

As modern concrete can break down in as little as 50 years, some **architects** are considering using Roman concrete for new building projects, such as a planned **tidal power** plant in Swansea, Wales.

WOW!

The Pantheon is the largest unreinforced concrete dome in the world. This means it does not contain any metal supports.

11

ROADS

While the Roman army helped to expand the empire, the construction of roads helped to maintain it. The Romans built a huge **network** of roads to link different parts of their empire. This made communication and trade much easier.

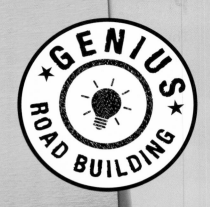

GENIUS
★ ★
ROAD BUILDING

Traveling at speed

Having a large network of well-built roads allowed soldiers and supplies to move quickly around the empire. Messengers with the official Roman postal service could travel as much as 100 miles (160 km) a day. If there was a rebellion against the Romans, the army could easily reach the rebels by traveling along Roman roads. This helped to keep conquered lands under control and maintain the empire.

This Roman road goes through the mountains of Spain. The Romans preferred to build roads on high ground, as they were less likely to be flooded. People traveling along the road were also safer, as they could see anyone approaching.

WOW!

At their peak, the Romans had built over 52,800 miles (85,000 km) of main roads, connecting the city of Rome with different parts of the empire.

Planning a road

The Romans were particular about the location of their roads. After they conquered new territory, they would send in mapmakers to study the area and plan routes for new roads. They built roads to link important points, such as towns and cities. For example, the Via Appia linked Rome to Brindisi, an important port. Most Roman roads were built in straight lines, as this covered the least distance.

Construction

The construction of a Roman road depended on its use. Busy roads were built to be much stronger than less-used roads. Road builders began by digging two shallow ditches on either side of the path of the road. Then, they built up the road above ground level between the ditches. The road was made from layers of **compacted** sand, crushed rock, and concrete, topped with large flat stones.

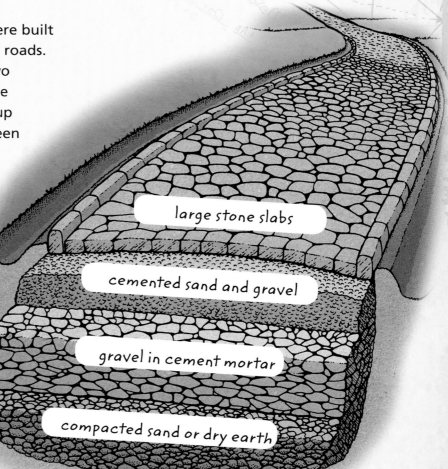

large stone slabs

cemented sand and gravel

gravel in cement mortar

compacted sand or dry earth

The road would slope down from the middle to the sides, so that water would run off into the ditches at the sides.

WATER

The Romans needed large quantities of water to supply cities and public baths. Luckily, they were excellent **engineers**, building aqueducts to bring clean water into their cities, and sewers to take dirty water away.

WOW!

It is estimated that Rome's 11 aqueducts brought about 265 gallons (1,000 liters) of clean water per person to the city every day. Rome had about one million citizens!

The Acqua Vergine aqueduct still brings water into Rome.

Bringing water

Aqueducts meant the Romans did not have to depend on a local freshwater supply. They could build cities in dry areas without much water. They could also supply large cities, such as Rome, with enough freshwater to support the population. In Rome, freshwater from aqueducts went into public fountains and drinking taps, where ordinary people collected water for everyday use. The wealthiest Romans had their own private water supply connected to their house.

(((BRAIN WAVE)))

The Romans built zigzags into some aqueducts. This slowed down the water so that it was more likely to drop its muddy **sediment**. This meant that the water was cleaner when it reached its destination.

14

Waste and sewage

The Romans built one of the earliest sewer systems in Rome, called the Cloaca Maxima. At first, the Cloaca Maxima was an open channel that drained water from the **marshland** where the Forum was built (see page 24). Later, it was covered over and used to carry dirty water from baths and public toilets into the Tiber River. The Romans built sewer systems in other parts of the empire, such as in Eboracum, which today is York, England.

Waste from public toilets fell into a trench beneath the seats.

Public baths

Having a reliable supply of water was vital for Roman public baths. Bathing was an important part of ancient Roman culture, and people would regularly visit public baths to wash, relax, and socialize. The Romans built baths across the empire. One of the largest were the Baths of Diocletian, which were built in Rome in around 300. They could fit 3,000 people and had swimming pools, warm and cold baths, steam rooms, and places to exercise.

Men and women used separate sections of the baths, as shown in this modern painting.

CALENDARS

The early Romans looked to the skies to help keep track of the days, months, and years. However, their first calendar, which was based on the cycles of the Moon, didn't really work. After some complicated calculations, the Romans produced a new, more accurate calendar, which is almost identical to the one that we use today.

GENIUS
★ LEAP YEAR ★

Calendar problems

The early Roman calendar was based on the cycles of the Moon. It only had 355 days in a year. This meant that the calendar slowly became out of **sync** with the seasons. Important moments in the farming year no longer matched the correct calendar month. By 100 B.C.E., the Roman calendar was three months out of sync.

All change

Around 40 B.C.E., the Roman general Julius Caesar ordered that the calendar be revised. He consulted a Greek **astronomer**, who suggested a version of the Egyptian solar calendar. The new Roman calendar had 365 days divided across twelve months. Every four years, there would be a leap year with one extra day added. Having leap years kept the new Roman calendar almost perfectly in sync.

Julius Caesar

Catching up

Before the Romans could start using their new calendar, they had to get the calendar days back on track. To do this, 46 B.C.E. had to have 445 days! The first 365-day year was 45 B.C.E. The new calendar made it much easier to keep track of important events and dates.

The ancient Greeks and Egyptians were advanced astronomers, and the Romans benefited from their knowledge.

TEST OF TIME

The Roman calendar was used until the Gregorian calendar was introduced by Pope Gregory XIII in 1582. The Gregorian calendar adjusted the Roman calendar slightly, making it even more accurate. Some Orthodox Christian Churches still use the Roman calendar to calculate the date of Easter.

WOW!

The seventh month in the new calendar was named "Julius," after Julius Caesar. Today, we call this month July.

The early Roman calendar was so out of sync, it showed the **harvest** to be happening in summer instead of autumn!

FOOD

There were many hungry mouths to feed in Rome and across the Roman Empire. Roman leaders realized that making sure people were fed well helped to keep the peace. However, the food that people ate depended greatly on their income.

An edible empire

The Romans ate foods from every region of their empire. Rich Romans enjoyed dates and pomegranates from northern Africa, high-quality olive oil from Spain, and spices from Asia. The Romans also collected grain from across the empire to feed the poor. Many of these foods had to be **preserved** so that they wouldn't go bad while being transported. The Romans pickled fruits and vegetables and salted meat so that they would last the journey.

Dates

Olives

Wheat

WOW!

Romans used *garum*, a sauce made from **fermented** fish, like we use ketchup. Historians think that *garum* factories were built outside cities, as the smell of the fermenting fish was so disgusting people couldn't live nearby!

Pomegranate

Everyday food

Most ordinary Romans could only afford a simple diet. They mostly ate barley, wheat, vegetables, and local olive oil, with occasional pieces of meat. This was a fairly balanced diet that kept most people healthy. In cities, most ordinary people lived in *insulae*, which were apartments with no full kitchen, only a one-pot stove over a fire. Only simple meals could be cooked at home.

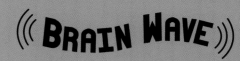

BRAIN WAVE

In cities, innkeepers and shopkeepers saw an opportunity to sell fast food to ordinary people who didn't have space to cook at home. They sold cheap, ready-to-eat meals, such as stews and sausages. Romans could eat in or take away to eat at home.

Political food

Food could sometimes be hard to come by, so Roman politicians often handed out food to win votes and approval. They also tried to persuade poor people to vote for them by lowering the price of grain or by handing out free grain. If politicians stopped giving out food, people protested. There were many poor people in Rome, so it would have been risky for politicians to make them all angry.

This is a Roman *thermopolium*, which was a type of fast-food restaurant. The holes in the counter would have been filled with jars of food.

This Roman painting shows bread being distributed to citizens.

THE LATIN LANGUAGE

Latin became the main language of the entire Roman Empire. After the empire ended, Latin continued to be used in science and other professions. It also developed into new languages.

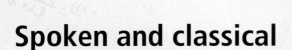

★GENIUS★
LANGUAGE THAT UNITED AN EMPIRE

Spoken and classical

The Romans used two different versions of Latin—spoken and classical. Each version had different words and grammar. Spoken Latin was used by ordinary people for everyday conversations and was rarely written down. Some modern languages, such as Italian and Spanish, developed from spoken Latin.

Classical Latin was taught at school and used to write important documents. The Romans created many different written works, ranging from stories to **philosophy** essays, historical accounts, and poetry. Much of what we know about ancient Rome is taken from these texts.

This engraving at the Colosseum in Rome is in classical Latin. We know much more about classical Latin than spoken Latin, as we have more written examples to study, such as the text on monuments.

Coming together

People in the Roman Empire were not required to speak Latin to become a Roman citizen. However, many people who lived in lands that came under Roman rule chose to learn Latin. Latin was used for government business and laws, so knowing it helped new people in the empire to blend into Roman society. A shared language allowed people from across the Roman Empire to communicate with each other and feel united.

TEST OF TIME

Today, many scientific, legal, and medical terms have Latin roots or are still written in Latin. For example, doctors use the instruction "nil per os" for a patient who should not eat anything. "Nil per os" means "nothing through the mouth" in Latin.

WOW!

The Latin alphabet is still used to write English and many other languages around the world. Today, it is the most widely used writing script in the world.

A replica of a Roman wax tablet. **Archaeologists** have found a few wax tablets with messages in spoken Latin, which have given us some clues about the language.

Writing it down

The Romans wrote on sheets made from papyrus plants. The papyrus sheets were very expensive to produce, so it was only used for the most important documents. The Romans came up with a clever solution for everyday writing. They filled wooden frames with solid wax and used a tool to carve messages into them. Later, they could melt the wax and erase the message, leaving the tablet ready to be used again.

GOVERNMENT

GENIUS ★
POWER-SHARING REPUBLIC

During the 500-year-long Roman Republic, the Romans were ruled over by a government made up of two **consuls** and a **council** called the Senate. This system stopped one ruler from becoming too powerful.

Changing consuls

The two elected consuls were in charge of the government and the army. To stop them from becoming too powerful, consuls only ruled for one year. Consuls usually came from wealthy families, but after 367 B.C.E., ordinary citizens could be elected. Later, it became law that one consul had to be an ordinary citizen.

The Roman consul Cicero talks to members of the Senate. Cicero served as consul in the year 63 B.C.E.

TEST OF TIME

The Roman Republic inspired the French Revolution (1789–1799), in which the French people overthrew the **monarchy** and started their own republic. France remains a republic today, ruled over by a president and a government. It does not have a monarchy.

The Senate

The consuls received advice from the Senate, a council of around 300 men. The Senate members came from the most important families in Rome. This gave them a huge amount of power, as they had many well-connected relatives and friends who the consuls did not want to annoy! For this reason, the consuls almost always took the advice of the Senate.

Republic to Empire

In 27 B.C.E., the Roman Republic became the Roman Empire. It was ruled over by a series of emperors. The emperor held all the power and made his own decisions about the empire. The Senate still existed, but it didn't have much power. Unlike during the Republic, the Senate was controlled by the emperor, rather than the Senate controlling the consuls. Some Roman emperors managed the empire well, while others were **corrupt** and used their position for their own personal benefit.

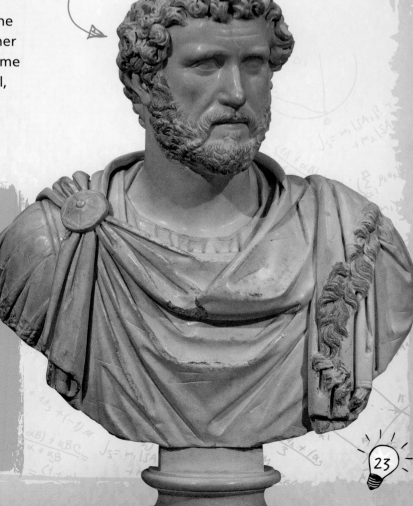

Antoninus Pius was the most peaceful Roman emperor. There were no major wars during his rule, which lasted from 138 to 161 C.E.

LAWS

Roman society was not equal. Women, enslaved people, and people who weren't Roman citizens did not enjoy the same treatment as rich men. However, the Romans did create laws to make things slightly fairer and to help stop the wealthy from abusing their power.

Unfair laws

In the early Roman Republic, only wealthy people could be judges. They made up the laws and chose how to use them. They also decided if someone was guilty and what their punishment should be. This gave judges power over ordinary people. They often abused the law to benefit themselves, make money, and punish their enemies.

The Twelve Tables were displayed in the Forum in Rome. During Roman times, this was a large public square between important government buildings.

The Twelve Tables

In 451 B.C.E., the Romans created the first law code, called the Twelve Tables. This was a list of twelve laws, written on bronze tablets and displayed publicly in Rome. These laws applied to everyone. As they were written down and could be seen by anyone, it was harder for rich people to change them. Over time, the Romans added more laws to their law code, covering many aspects of life and business. The rules on who could be a judge also changed to include any free man, rich or poor.

Punishments

Romans gave out serious punishments to people accused of breaking the law. They hoped that these punishments would be a warning to others who were tempted to break the law. Many crimes were punished by death. However, the way in which people were killed depended on who they were. Wealthy people sentenced to death were executed in private, while ordinary people were killed publicly. Enslaved people were often killed during gladiator matches (see page 29).

(see page 29)

(((BRAIN WAVE)))

The Twelve Tables created the need for lawyers, a job that had not really existed before. Roman lawyers helped people to **interpret** and understand Roman law. Some Romans also worked as law experts, who studied laws and tested them against imaginary cases to make sure they were working well.

One Roman form of execution was to throw the person sentenced to death off a cliff.

CITY SERVICES

In a large city such as Rome, the risk of fire and crime was fairly high. The world's first fire department also acted as a police force, helping to stop fires and keep criminals off the streets.

The lower floors of insulae were more expensive as they had larger rooms and were less of a fire risk.

At home

Many people in Rome lived in *insulae* in narrow, crowded streets. The bottom floors of these apartment blocks were made from brick or stone, while the top floors were made from wood. People in these apartments used oil lamps for light, and open fires for cooking and heat. For people living on the top wooden floors, this was a serious fire risk. As well, the buildings were so close together that a fire in one apartment could quickly spread into a huge citywide fire.

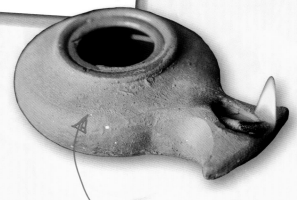

Romans burned plant oil, such as olive oil, in oil lamps.

Vigiles

To prevent the risk of a serious fire in Rome, the emperor Augustus started a fire department in 6 C.E. The fire department employed professional firemen called *vigiles*. Their name came from the Latin word "vigil," meaning alert and watchful. Over 7,000 *vigiles* patrolled the streets of Rome, keeping watch for fires.

On patrol

When the *vigiles* were not putting out fires, they had time to patrol the city at night, acting as a police force. They kept an eye out for thieves, and handled low-level crimes, such as fighting. This helped to make the streets of Rome safer.

(((BRAIN WAVE)))

In case of a fire, *vigiles* could use a "fire engine" to put out the flames. This was a large water pump on a wagon, pulled by horses. They used the pump to get water from a water source near the fire. Then, they brought buckets of water to put out the fire.

TEST of TIME

The *vigiles* were the world's first fire department. Today, over 2,000 years later, almost every town and city in the world has a fire department with firefighters and equipment to put out dangerous fires.

The emperor was protected by a group of soldiers called the Praetorian Guard. In the case of a serious crime, the Praetorian Guard could be called on to help the vigiles.

SHOW TIME!

Roman emperors were keen to keep poor people entertained, as they were less likely to **revolt** when they were distracted. They built huge buildings where free entertainment took place, such as **chariot** races and gladiator fights.

GENIUS ENTERTAINERS

Big buildings

The buildings where Roman entertainment took place had to be large enough to fit huge crowds. The Colosseum, where spectators watched gladiator matches, could seat over 50,000 people. The Circus Maximus in Rome was a huge chariot-racing stadium. It had seating for over 150,000 people.

Risk of danger

Roman entertainment was designed to be exciting and dangerous, to keep people interested. In Roman chariot races, 12 chariots raced seven laps around a huge track. Each chariot racer tried to get the best position near the barrier in the center. Crashes at high speed were very common.

The chariots were as light as possible to make it easier for the horses to pull them. However, this meant there wasn't much protection for the driver if they crashed into the central barrier or another chariot.

Gory sports

Roman crowds enjoyed watching violent matches. Gladiators would fight each other until one of them either surrendered or died. Spectators could also watch criminals receive punishments, such as having to fight lions or bears without weapons or armor. If the criminal managed to kill the animal, another would be released for the criminal to fight.

(((BRAIN WAVE)))

The Romans used advertising to attract large crowds to gladiator events. They painted ads on buildings a few days before the show. The ads mentioned the names of the gladiators who would be fighting, the style of fighting, and when and where the event would take place.

WOW!

Each type of gladiator had a different fighting style. A *retiarius* gladiator fought with a net and a **trident**. An *andabata* gladiator is thought to have fought on horseback.

A *secutor* gladiator fights a *retiarius* gladiator. Secutor gladiators were specially trained to fight *retiarius* gladiators. They carried a large shield and short sword.

trident

GLOSSARY

aqueduct A structure for carrying water across land

archaeologist A person who studies ancient cultures by examining sites and artifacts

archer A person who shoots with a bow and arrow

architect Someone who designs and constructs buildings

astronomer Someone who studies planets and the stars

cavalry Soldiers who fought on horseback

chariot A horse-drawn vehicle used in ancient warfare and racing

city-state A city and the area around it that function as an independent country

civil war A war between citizens of the same country

civilization The stage of a human society, such as its culture and way of life

climate The weather conditions in a particular area

compacted Packed tightly

consul During the Roman Republic, one of two people in charge of running the government and the army

corrupt To act dishonestly to gain money

council A group of people who advise and manage a city or country

culture The beliefs and customs of a group of people

empire A group of states or countries ruled by a single authority

engineer A person who designs and builds machines and structures

fermented When food has been broken down by bacteria into chemicals

formation A formal arrangement of troops

gladiator A man trained to fight other men or wild animals in an arena

harvest To gather a crop

impenetrable Something that is impossible to break into

interpret To understand the meaning of something

javelin A spear that is thrown in battle or competitions

legacy Something handed down from the past

marshland Land that is always wet or flooded

mineral Solid substances that make up sand, soil, and rocks

mold A frame that gives shape to something

monarchy Rule by a king or queen

mortar A substance used to hold bricks or stones together

myth An invented story related to history

natural resources Materials or substances from nature that can be used to earn money

network A system of connected departments working together

philosophy The study of thought and knowledge

pirate A person who attacks and robs ships at sea

preserved When something is kept in its current state by being prevented from decaying

republic A country whose leader is elected by the people

revolt When a large number of people protest against their leaders and refuse to be ruled by them

sediment Sand or grit that settles to the bottom of a liquid

sync Short for synchronize, to happen at the same time

tactically When soldiers move in war in a carefully planned and organized way

tidal power Converting the energy from waves into electricity

trident A weapon that consists of a pole with three metal points on the end

versatile Able to be used in many different ways

TIMELINE

600 B.C.E.   Rome is a city-state ruled by kings.

509 B.C.E.   The last Roman king is overthrown and the Roman Republic starts.

27 B.C.E.   The Roman Empire begins and the first emperor, Augustus, begins his rule.

117 C.E.   The Roman Empire is at its greatest size, ruling over areas including what is now Spain, Britain, northern Africa, and Turkey.

395   The Roman Empire has officially split in half.

476   The Western Roman Empire ends.

The city of Rome today.

INDEX

LEARNING MORE

Websites

www.historyforkids.net/ancient-rome.html

www.dkfindout.com/us/history/ancient-rome/

https://kids.kiddle.co/Roman_Empire

Books

Malam, John. *Ancient Rome Inside Out*. Crabtree Publishing, 2017.

Nardo, Don. *Daily Life in Ancient Rome*. Heinemann, 2015.

Spilsbury, Louise. *Forensic Investigations of the Romans*. Crabtree Publishing, 2019.